A Short History of Race Americas

For Young Readers Of All Ages
by Curran Jeffery

Part One

There was a time,
A long time ago,
When there were
No humans, male or female
In the Americas,
Either North or South.

About 18,000 years ago or there about, hunter/gatherer clans of humans from Asia started to cross the land bridge that existed between what we call Alaska and Siberia. This land bridge existed at the end of the last Ice Age before the melting ice flooded it out of existence.

Looking for better hunting, possibly following herds of Elk or Deer and following the lush abundant forests, these were the first Americans. They were Siberian-Asian, probably short brown people, muscular, hardy and agile. Over hundreds and thousands of years they moved up and down the coast and spine of what we would call North and South America. They weren't the light skinned Europeans or the dark skinned Africans. Those people would arrive later. Much later. The first Native Americans had the two continents to themselves for thousands of years. At first, their small bands, usually just extended families, slipped into the forests, mountains, prairies, deserts of Americas and learned to survive. They raised families, hunted, some discovered farming. They fought wars over hunting grounds and territory. They made peace. Powerful rituals and wonderful and frightening legends of the spirits explained the mysteries of life.

Clans grew into tribes. Tribes into nations. Each with their own language, culture, sacred story and way of life, pride and honor. All these peoples had great awe and wonder for father sky and mother earth. This was their sacred space which gave them life.

There was war as tribes and clans would fight each other for control of the resources. There would also be peace and farming and trade. The hunter/gatherers were ruled by elders and shamans who understood the magic of the forests. Warrior peoples were ruled by strong chiefs who invoked divine powers for victory. Farm people with towns and then cities were ruled by priests who understood the magic of the seasons and could invoke the rain and the sun.

The Mayan Civilization lasted over 3000 years in Central America with huge cities, magnificent architecture, mathematics and astronomy. They had a complex written language that included pictures and an alphabet. The Aztec Civilization which came much later had a picture based written language but not an alphabet. Both the Mayans and later the Aztecs had a complex religion of gods and rituals which included blood sacrifice. The Aztecs would wage war to capture prisoners for their thirsty gods. It was brutal.

In the Andes Mountains in what is today Peru, the Timanku people who would become the Incas began creating their culture which would eventually build a magnificent sacred city atop a mountain built in stone without benefit of the wheel. A major accomplishment.

In North America the ancestors of the Pueblo peoples and the Mississippian People were establishing large towns of well planned elaborate construction, irrigation, farming, and trade. The forest peoples continued their earth-centered hunting culture which had sustained their people for thousands of generations.

In 985 C.E. Eric the Red—a Viking from Norway—settled in Greenland. In 1001 C.E. his son Leif Erickson arrived on the coast of what would become Newfoundland. This is the first contact of the American continent with Caucasian Europeans. The Vikings established a settlement which lasted many years but it did not survive the harsh winters or the long distances.

The Second encounter of the Americas with Caucasian Europeans was in 1492 C. E. on the island the native inhabitants called Guanahani. These were the Taino people of the Bahamas. They were peaceful, friendly and curious. But it soon became clear that the Spanish led by Christopher Columbus were not to be trusted. Several of the Tainos were taken forcefully back to Spain. The Spanish were looking for a sea passage to the Orient for the spice trade. Failing in that, they were looking for gold, silver, and land for plantations and people to work the mines and the crops. Columbus' four trips to the Americas began the Spanish conquest which was a disaster for the Native peoples but provided immense wealth for Spain. The first meeting of the Native American (originally Asian) and European peoples in the Americas did not go well. On his third trip to the Americas, Columbus returned with many enslaved natives which were presented to Queen Isabella. She immediately freed them and ordered them to be returned to their homes. The Queen had serious reservation about forced labor from people she saw as her newest subjects. She consulted her court and the Church but by 1503, enslavement of native people was a reality in most of the Spanish territories but she did not approve. Her will asks that her successors treat her native subjects fairly. Her voice was not heard.

The Spanish Cavalry terrorized the native warriors. European armor was the best and could deflect the arrows and war clubs of the Americans. The Spanish long swords made by the skilled black smiths of Toledo in Spain could decapitate heads like swinging a golf club. The Muskets of 1500 were awkward and not very effective but made a loud noise that convinced the native peoples that the Spanish fought with thunder.

The defeat of the first American people by the Spanish was largely due to European military superiority but the fatal blow was from small pox, measles, and influenza all of which traveled to the Americas on the Spanish ships. The Americas had not seen these diseases before thus no natural immunity. People started to die in droves: whole villages, whole cities depopulated. Millions died. Mayan, Aztec, and Incan civilizations came to an abrupt end. Soon the same fate would strike the peoples of North America.

In 1496, Diego Columbus, the brother of Christopher established Santo Domingo in what would become the Dominican Republic. This was the first secure European settlement in the Americas. By 1515 the conquest of Cuba was complete and the town of Havana established. In 1519 the Conquistador Hernando Cortez lands with men and cannons on the coast of Mexico. At first the Aztec Emperor Montezuma welcomes him thinking he is the returning god Quetzalcoatl. Cortez turns on him. The Aztecs resist for a year but the Spanish take control of Mexico. The conquistadors settle on land granted to them by the Crown for the conquest.   Many Aztecs become forced laborers.   The Priests and Friars built chapels and begin the conversion of the native peoples to the one true faith of Spanish Roman Catholicism.   The Aztec and Mayan gods are treated as superstition and devil worship. The Friars were horrified by the human sacrifice. At first, the conversions are mostly forced. The Bishop Diego de Landa burned all the Mayan books he could find and burned them in front of a church. Only four of the books survive and the ability to read the Mayan written language was lost for over 400 years. After decades of work by linguists and scholars the code has been broken and the Mayan written language can be read again. There are today hundreds of thousands of Mayans still living on their ancestral lands, still speaking Mayan dialects.

Historians have often wondered about how quickly the Mexican people converted to Roman Catholicism. It happened in one or two generations. Many pre-conquest traditions survive.   The Virgin of Guadalupe can be seen as the reincarnation of the Aztec Mother Goddess. The Blood of the Cross can be seen as replacing the need for human sacrifice.   Indeed God Himself becomes human and is sacrificed for the salvation of everyday people.   This isn't that far from Aztec religion where gods require human blood to sustain humanity.

It wasn't long before Spanish ships were taking gold and silver treasure back to Spain, the mines being worked by the forced labor of the captured people but traveling with the Spanish sailors were also tuberculous and syphilis, two diseases that had not been seen in Europe before. What goes around, comes around.

When the friars and the Spanish army arrived in the Land of the Pueblos, they were greeted, and offered food and water and a place to stay.   The friars started to talk the one true church and the soldiers built a fort. At first, friars were amazed at how receptive the people were to their message. The Pueblo People were very spiritual with a special relationship with the spirit of the earth and sky and the ancestors. They saw themselves as part of a Great Mystery. Their religion was very ancient but also open to new ways. They added Jesus and Mary to their practice. When the friars realized that they were a mere addition and not a replacement, they cracked down. When people were caught practicing the old religion, they were tortured and often killed. Spanish Pueblo relations turned violent. In 1680, the pueblos went to war. Over 400 Spanish were killed including most of the priests and friars and the rest forced out of the Rio Grande Valley, back into Mexico. They returned 12 years later with a heavy military escort and never left again.

In September 1565, the Admiral Mendez de Aviles came ashore with settlers, soldiers and supplies and founded St. Augustine in what would become Florida. St. Augustine is the oldest European town in North America. However, the oldest town in North America is the Acoma Pueblo in New Mexico which was founded 1000 years ago and has been continuously inhabited ever since.

The first successful English settlement in North America was on a river that feeds into Chesapeake Bay called Jamestown (1607). The previous settlement, Roanoke (1585,) had disappeared without a trace before their supply ships got back from England. It's speculated that the Roanoke settlers had absorbed into the local tribes to escape famine from a severe drought. Tree rings tell that those years had a serious lack of rain. Food and fresh water would have been scarce.

The Powhatan welcomed the English as a chance to trade for steel and iron tools. But it soon became clear that the English wanted to control the food supply and the land. Hostilities broke out. The lingering drought may have been responsible at least in part, for the tension. The Powhatans and the English would have been competing for the same sources of food and fresh water. Over half the English died the first year. But unlike Roanoke, Jamestown survived and soon began to prosper. Native Americans were pushed back. Tobacco farms appeared to ship tobacco back to England where it had a growing popularity.

This is the story of the first two branches of humanity to live in what we call the Americas: Native Americas descended from Asia who arrived thousands of years ago and Europeans who arrived from the other side of the Atlantic just a few hundred years ago. In 1619 Jamestown received it's first Africans, probably from Angola, on a ship of an English privateer. Twenty Negros put to work on the tobacco farms. Many White Englishmen worked on the farms as indentured servants. Seven years of labor would pay for their passage and their training and they would be freed. The first Africans in Jamestown were treated as "indentured servants." At the end of seven years some were freed and some were not. The farms needed labor. The Atlantic slave trade was about come to the English colonies. In 1640, the Virginia Governors Council declared that John Punch, a Black man who considered himself an indentured servant was actually a life-long slave. This was the beginning of legal, race based slavery in English North America. There were already Africans enslaved in Spanish Florida in and around St. Augustine

A year after the arrival of Africans in Jamestown, the English Puritans landed in the land of the Wampanoag people far to the north after being blown off course by Atlantic storms. Their destination had been Virginia but landed in December in what would become Massachusetts. They spent the first winter on their ship anchored near the shore. They suffered terribly in the cold. Many died of disease and hunger. They persevered. They saw no sign of the people who they knew were probably watching them. The local tribe had been hit hard by an epidemic and under threat from the Narragansett who lived to the West. Massasoit, the chief of the Wampanoag thought the new arrivals might be of help. After several months he sent Samoset to speak to the Puritans. The Puritans were amazed. Samoset spoke English and asked for a beer. He had learned some English from English fishing fleets. But there was still confusion. Samoset came back a week later with Squanto. This was in March 1621. The Puritans were even more amazed. Squanto spoke fluent English and seemed familiar with the ways of the English. He had been kidnaped by the Explorer Thomas Hunt and taken to Spain as a slave. He was "bought" by Monks who educated him in European ways. He was sent to England, learned English, secured a voyage back to his world only to find his village had been wiped out by the epidemic. (The diseases which were affecting Native peoples were probably of European origins from the sailors on the fishing boats.)

Squanto along with Samoset, brokered peace with the Puritans. They taught the Puritans how to grow native crops. They showed the Puritans the secrets of survival in a forest land. (The seeds the Puritans brought with them failed to sprout.) William Bradford, the Puritan governor, credits Squanto with the Survival of the first Puritan community. Relations with local tribes were good for a few years but the arrival of many more Puritans and the establishment of other settlements created tensions with and among the Puritans and the various tribes. Violence broke out in the 1630's and in Chief Metacom's War in 1675. It was Brutal with atrocities on both sides that ended in the complete defeat of the tribes. The Puritans began forging an identity independent of being English. This was the beginning of "White America." The Native Americans were pushed further

West where the fur trade between the tribes, the French and the Dutch was getting very competitive and would lead to the French and Indian War.

By 1650 the Atlantic Slave Trade was creating tremendous human suffering as Europeans bought into the slave trade of West Africa. Prisoners of warring tribes were often captured and kept as slaves within the tribes. This was not the dehumanizing chattel slavery that would emerge with Europeans but a traditional POW system of African Culture. The POW's, although prisoners, were treated with some dignity and respect. The first Portuguese explorers traded for these POW's who were then treated as property to be shipped off to forced labor in the America's. It was profitable and soon bands of European backed bounty hunters were capturing people to be sold into the dehumanizing Atlantic slave trade.

Although ancient hunter/gather cultures probably did not practice slavery, the practice of forced labor has been a part of most human history since. In the Atlantic slave trade, it took a truly sinister turn for the worse which left deep wounds on the soul of the modern world that are still in need of healing. People were kidnapped from their homelands, forced to forget their families, language, culture even their religion, to spend weeks chained on cramped slave ships with barely enough food and water and only a bucket for a toilet which was often out of reach. Disease was rampant. Many died in route. In the Americas, they were sold like cattle to work forced labor on farms, mines, kitchens and plantations. Europeans involved in the trade did not see these people as having dignity therefore it was OK to treat them as less then human. This was race-based forced labor. It is estimated that over 10 million people were removed from Africa to the Americas as slaves: 40% to Brazil where conditions on the plantations were brutal, 50% to the British West Indies,

French Territories and Spanish Empire, and 10% to the British Atlantic colonies. These would become the African Americans of today's United States.

Most 21st Century people think of Old Africa as a monolithic primitive and very simple world. Nothing could be further from the truth. Like the pre-European Americas, Africa had a long history of Empires, cities, nations, cultures, languages and religions. It wasn't all just ancient Egypt. There are several West African Empires with great art and culture and histories, the best known being the Mali Empire from the 1200's to the 1600's and the Yoruba culture which produced exquisite sculpture in bronze. Most Africans forced into chattel slavery were from West Africa.

It is now well into the 1600's. In the Salons of Paris, London, Amsterdam, and Prague, Renaissance Humanism is evolving into the Age of the Enlightenment. In 1686 Isaac Newton published his "Principia Mathematica" which makes it clear that reason and logic, not the faith of the church, are the new normal. This paves the way for respect, tolerance, compassion and the ideals of the French and American revolutions. But the world has a long way to go. In 1776 Thomas Jefferson would write "We hold these truths to be self-evident: That all men are created equal," knowing full well the contradiction that his large farms were worked by slaves. It would take another century and a brutal war to work this out.

The first opposition to slavery in the English colonies came in 1688 from the Quakers in Pennsylvania. Some Quakers owned slaves and many other Quakers felt that was incompatible with the Gospels. Francis Daniel Pastorious penned the Quaker Petition Against Slavery which affirmed the rights of all human beings. Although the Quaker leadership did not take action until much later, this early and forceful anti-slavery petition became the inspiration for the later abolitionist movement.

The Colony of Georgia was founded in 1733. The founder James Edward Olgethorpe refused to allow South Carolina to bring slaves into Georgia saying that slavery violated the principles that brought us together and that it was wrong to inflict misery on Africans. Olgethorpe envisioned Georgia as a haven for England's worthy poor and disadvantaged. His vision didn't last. Gradually slavery and the plantation system prevailed.

The history of human forced labor in the Americas was all over the map. Native peoples of what would become Brazil would enslave prisoners of war. When the Portuguese arrived, they would trade POW's to the Europeans for iron and steel tools. But the native forced labor was not enough for large sugar plantations which emerged as the base of the Brazilian economy. Africans were brought in. African forced labor on the sugar plantations was notoriously brutal with a short life span that kept up a constant demand for more people to be brought from Africa. It is estimated that 4,000,000 Africans were brought captive to Brazil before they abolished slavery in 1888. Brazil was the last country in the Americas to abolish forced labor.

The Spanish Royal Court led by Queen Isabella did not support enslaving native peoples but it happened anyway. African forced labor was seen as an alternative. Bartolome de las Casas, a Dominican Friar very opposed to abuse of native peoples even supported that alternative till he realized that it was equally cruel. He remained a vocal voice against the sin of slavery but the economic realities that made forced labor profitable kept all attempts to stop it from succeeding. Roughly 2,000,000 Africans were brought to the Atlantic colonies for involuntary forced labor. There was a small but growing opposition. Some form of slavery existed in all the Atlantic colonies in the early 1700's. In 1780, largely because of the Quakers, Pennsylvania passed An Act for the Gradual Abolition of Slavery but the constitution of the new nation allowed the importation of slaves until 1808. In 1783 the Massachusetts Supreme Court ruled that forced labor was incompatible with the State constitution. This was the emerging pattern: the Northern States would come to oppose chattel slavery and the Southern states would embrace it. The Southern Slave holding elites refused to consider any talk of compromise or gradual emancipation. The abolitionists insisted on an immediate end to all human beings being held as property. The tragedy was that the Southern economy had become totally dependent on forced labor. No one seemed to see a way out. And the way out would be war over Union and Slavery.

In the Southwest, The Pueblo Revolt of 1680 had an unexpected radical impact on tribes such as the Navajo, Cheyenne, Comanche, Sioux and the many tribes along the Missouri River. When the Spanish were driven from the Pueblo lands they left behind their livestock. The Pueblo People had no use for the horses which they would let roam wild. This became new "technology" that changed the way people lived. The Navajos adopted the sheep and learned how to spin and weave the wool. The mustangs, now wild, grew into great herds. The plains people would capture, tame and learn how to ride them: the beginning of the great "horse culture" of the plains people. Prior to the Spanish horse, the tribes were hunter/gatherers with a real challenge to survive. It wasn't easy for a band of hunters on foot to take down a buffalo but they did. Now mounted hunters could take as many as the tribe would need. Mounted warriors could take on neighboring tribes in battle for land and resources. Later, the mounted warriors would offer stubborn resistance to the advancing American army.

But it wasn't all war and conflict. The Great Law of Peace of the Iroquois Nations which had maintained peace between once warring tribes for generations influenced Ben Franklin and other colonial founding fathers. The Iroquois Nation was a federation of five tribes, once all bitter enemies who had come together under an enlightened elder and worked out what in effect was a constitution that established the rights of tribes under a leadership dedicated to cooperation and peace. It had been working for generations. This Iroquois Peace of the Five Nations inspired the men who were working on what would become the American Constitution.

In the Pacific Northwest, the mild climate, abundant Salmon, and forests enabled the original people to develop elaborate arts, houses, totems, costumes rituals and great ocean going cedar canoes. They were flourishing when the early Spanish explorers arrived with small pox. The reduction of population was as high as 90% in some areas which made it easier for European settlers to move into the area. In the early and mid 1800's the legendary Chief Seattle maintained a somewhat peaceful relationship with the Anglo-Americans which got the town of Seattle named after him. There is no documentation for his legendary speech which was no doubt embellished over time but there is no doubt that he stood for respecting the earth and native peoples. After his death, his people were sent to reservations.

Much further to the north the Inuit and related tribes adapted to life near the Arctic Circle learning to build ice houses that protected them from the bitter cold and to survive on hunting seals through the ice, fishing, whaling, and hunting polar bears. Recent climate changes are seriously impacting and threatening their way of life.

So here we are in the beginning of the modern world, the late 1700's and the early 1800's. Human beings have completely populated the once un-human inhabited continents. Three major human races are here. Native Americans, descended from Asian/Siberian ancestors who crossed the now submerged ancient land bridge. The Euro-Americans descended from the Spanish, English, Dutch, and French who arrived over the Atlantic only about 500 years ago. African- Americans who were kidnapped, stripped of their identity and shipped to the America's for involuntary forced labor. These human beings who inhabit the Americas have built great nations, great cities, great science, music, art and even put a man on the moon. Why has there been so much suffering, fear, pain, and death? To understand this let's go way back to the very beginning of being human hundreds of thousands of years ago.

The human imagination is an energy of deep wisdom that defies understanding. All the peoples of earth have found sacred stories to guide them through the overwhelming challenges they have faced and to give courage and wisdom and faith and meaning. We are meaning seeking people. The Africans who arrived in the Atlantic colonies were stripped of their religions, either Islam or the native spirituality of West Africa with its majestic sky God and angel spirits. Newly arrived Africans heard the Exodus of the Hebrew Moses and embraced his story. It gave them meaning, strength, and courage. They embraced Jesus with his message of Love and Forgiveness.   The Black

Church was born from in the bowels of the slave ships. One of their grandsons proclaimed "I have been to the Mountain top and I have seen the Promised Land."

Our sacred stories are what make us human. But they also make us less than human when we abuse them: when we turn them against each other. What is this "us vs. them" thing that drives human history? It is our deep human nature. It began when the first humans were emerging into to awareness. It was "us' versus "them." It is "in group" versus "out group." It's what some call the law of the jungle or the survival of the fittest. We learned to love and help our own kind and be hostile to those who aren't like us. Compassion and aggression emerged in human nature hand-in-hand, because they were both necessary for survival. It is buried in our bones. We learned to love our own and fear those who were not us. Each of us is a part of that story. No one is exempt. It is still with us today. It is dualistic, "Us Vs. Them" thinking.

Just as wise elders led the warring tribes of the Iroquois into finding ways to live in peace as Five Nations, sages, prophets, saints and elders in many Sacred Stories have shown ways out of the cycle of violence, fear and hatred. It started with the Chinese philosopher Confucius who taught "Don't do to others what you don't want done to you." Confucius lived centuries ago when ancient China was torn by warlords. His ideas helped people to expand their idea of to whom they had to be nice and to reduce the violence. But it didn't stop. There was always another enemy just over the horizon. The Buddha in Hindu India spoke of the oneness of all creation and of all beings. He taught compassion and meditation to find inner peace which could then become the peace of the world. He ushered in an unparalleled era of peace and prosperity for all of India. But it too didn't last. Moses in the Torah wrote "Love thy neighbor as thy self" but it seemed the understanding of who was your neighbor stopped at your boundaries. Then Jesus taught to love your enemies, pray for those who curse you and in proclaiming "The Kingdom of God," broke down all sorts of barriers between humans. The Sacred Stories kept expanding to include an ever growing circle. When you stop thinking in terms of "us vs. them" and start seeing all people as part of the great story, things start to change...even the story can change.

A Short History of Race In America: Part Two

The history of race in America is both part of a great story and an ugly story. It is full of hope and promise, death and despair.

The first Asians from China began to arrive in the 1840's attracted by the California Gold Rush and jobs on the Transcontinental Railroad. The men came without their wives, sending money home and planning to return home. But the economic hardships and political unrest in China made starting a new life in America very appealing. By the 1880's, there were a 100,000 Chinese living and working in the USA. We have already seen how the clash of peoples of a different appearance and a different culture can result in racial tension. There were serious massacres of Chinese miners along the Snake River in Oregon and in 1871 an anti-Chinese riot in Los Angeles. Some of the perpetrators were convicted but released by the courts on technicalities. Violence against the Chinese, like violence against Blacks, was acceptable to many White people and those to whom the violence was not acceptable mostly kept quiet.

Immigration in the 1800's was bringing many new people to the Americas, many were Roman Catholic, not Protestant English. They were Irish, Italian, Polish, and Jewish. The native-born Protestant English-Americans of Philadelphia feared and despised the Irish Catholics. This conflict goes back for generations in the British Isles. The Bible Riots of the 1840's

(Philadelphia) went on for days, resulted in 30 deaths with two Roman Catholic churches and convents burned to the ground along with dozens of Irish homes. It was over the Irish Catholic Bishop asking that Irish children in the public schools be able to read from a Catholic Bible rather than the King James Bible. The Anglo-Saxon Protestants accused the Catholics of throwing out the Bible.

Jews, Italians, and Poles all faced similar opposition in New York, Chicago and St. Louis. But the new Europeans were white and looked the other way when it came to the forced labor of African slaves in the Southern states.

The New York Anti-Draft of 1863 started out as a protest by low income Euro-Americans including the Irish against the fact that the rich could pay a fee of $300 and be exempt from the draft. It turned into a race riot that lasted three days, resulted in 105 dead, including 12 lynchings, the burning of several blocks including homes of the rich elites as well as those of African Americans. The working class Whites accused freed Negroes of taking their jobs and that it was a rich man's war. The New York Militia had been called to assist at Battle of Gettysburg which is why the New York police were overwhelmed. As soon as the New York State Militia got back to the city, things settled down.

The Battle of Gettysburg was a turning point in the war. After Lee's defeat at Gettysburg events started to go well for the Union. If General Meade had pursued the Army of Northern Virginia Lee might have surrendered much sooner.

War is the ultimate "us vs. them" human behavior. No one really wins. The stage is just set for the next battle. The Civil War ended legal slavery in United States but set the stage for the "Jim Crow" laws. The assassination of President Abraham Lincoln silenced the one voice that spoke clearly for reconciliation and the only one with a clear plan for healing the wounds of war. With his death, the plans for reconstruction disintegrated into chaos. You had nearly 3,000,000 suddenly freed people with no clear plan for absorbing these workers into a paid workforce or a farming economy. Chaos and corruption became the norm. After the failure of Reconstruction, the Jim Crow Laws separated the races in most aspects of life from stores, drinking fountains, restrooms, hotels, schools and even churches. Convict leasing replaced slavery in several southern states. A young man, almost always Black but could be poor White or Native American, anyone considered an undesirable, could be stopped, arrested and convicted on charges ranging from vagrancy, drunk and disorderly to trespassing and sentenced for several months of hard labor. These "chain gangs" were leased out to plantations, railroads, construction crews, coal mines. The lessees were not supervised by the state and conditions were minimal. Sometimes less then minimal. There was no compensation but it wasn't forever.

Mob lynchings were the real terror used by White communities against freed Blacks. Starting in the 1880's and continuing well into the 20th Century, a mere rumor of a black man making an unwanted advance on a White woman could trigger a mob enforced lynching. The NAACP estimates there were 3440 racially motivated lynchings in the Southern states between 1882 and 1968. Some were convicted criminals who were turned over to mobs rather than go through the courts. But most of the victims never had a chance to prove their innocence. In 1955 14 year old Emmett Till, visiting from Chicago, was lynched in Mississippi for "offending a white woman" in a grocery store. His murderers were found not guilty by an all White jury. Since double jeopardy applied to the case and they could not be tried again for the same crime, they confessed to the killing in an article in <u>Look</u> Magazine in 1956. The outrage over this incident fueled the Montgomery Bus Boycott and the emerging Civil Rights Movement.

The end of slavery did not end the racial oppression of African Americans. It just changed the way it worked. Conditions for enslaved American's in the 1800's up until the end of the Civil War were challenging and difficult but simple. The African people were property with no rights what so ever except for what their owners might give them. There were two kinds of owners with lots of variations in between: cruel and soft. The cruel would use flogging, frequent sellings and even hunger for control. "Soft" masters had a humane streak, would respect families and avoid flogging. They would view slavery as a way of bringing civilization and Christianity to the "rescued savages." The quality of life of an enslaved person would depend on their owner and also their skills. Field hands and cotton pickers were the worse off. Someone who had obtained skills as a carpenter, blacksmith, cook, house servant, seamstress, cobbler, or horse trainer could fare bit better but it was a hard life lacking in justice throughout the Southern states.

On the great plains, the new horse culture matured and Native tribes were powerful and aggressive in defending their buffalo hunting grounds against the Euro-Americans coming in wagon trains to fence, graze and farm. There were attacks, violence and death. In 1876, the Northern Cheyenne and the Arapaho defeated the US 7th Cavalry at the Battle of Little Big Horn in the Montana Territory. Native Americans called this the Battle of The Greasy Grass. It was the last major victory of Native Americans against the US Cavalry. Three hundred and twenty three US soldiers were killed or severely wounded. As the Euro-Americans moved west the plains people were pushed back and moved to reservations. They were coerced into treaties granting them land on the reservations to sustain their way of life. These treaties were never honored and the amount of land was frequently reduced as more Euro-Americans moved into the area. By the 1880's hunger and despair were the norm in native communities. By 1890 the situation was desperate. In South Dakota nearly 300 Lakota people, mostly woman and children died in The Battle of Wounded Knee in the starving winter from a hail of gunfire from US troops who thought they were under attack. Eye witness accounts are conflicting. There is no way to know how the first shot was fired but the US Officers lost control of their men who went on a rampage and killed any Lakota they could find including woman and children. The Lakota people had been traveling under a white flag of truce. This was the last major military action against Native American people by the US Army. After this. life on the reservation became even more difficult. Children were forced into reservation schools where they could only speak English, had to dress like Euro-Americans and not study their own culture but learn the new ways.

In the cities of the East, New York, Boston, Pittsburg, Detroit, Chicago industry was flourishing. There were jobs; steel mills, factories, meat packers, and rail roads. They paid better than share-cropping in the South. Starting about 1916 onward, thousands of rural workers, White and Black but mostly Black moved North. Called the Great Migration an estimated 2 million African Americans moved to the cities of the North and the West seeking new opportunities. Soon large comfortable African American neighborhoods appeared in all these cities. There was White resistance, racial tension and violence. In 1921, the prosperous African community of Tulsa was burned to the ground with over 30 dead and 800 injured.

The National Association for the Advancement of Colored People was formed in 1909 by both White and Black people to work for justice without discrimination. African American leaders such as Booker T. Washington and W.E.B. DuBois, the first African American PhD from Harvard, worked hard to move the United States away from its racist past. Despite the violence and the tension there was some hope during the Roaring 20's with the Harlem Renaissance, the poetry of Langston Hughes, the novels of Zora Neale Hurston, the Jazz of Louis Armstrong, Duke Ellington, Ella Fitzgerald and so many others. Then the Great Depression hit all Americans hard followed by World War II. At the end of the great Depression and just before the War, African American vocalist Marian Anderson, a very accomplished classical singer, was to perform at Constitution Hall in Washington DC. The Daughters of the American Revolution refused to allow a Black singer to perform on that stage to an integrated audience. First Lady Eleanor Roosevelt intervened and arranged for her to sing an Easter concert on the steps of the Lincoln memorial to an audience of 75,000 and a radio audience of millions.

The segregation of American life spilled into the war. African American troops were assigned to segregated units and Japanese- American citizens who were born in the USA were sent to detention camps. Still, the all Black Tuskegee Airman of the 15th Air Force flew thousands of air attacks in the liberation of Europe and the Navajo Code Talkers kept the Japanese military from cracking the Allied codes in the Pacific. The war laid the groundwork for the post war civil rights movement. It didn't happen overnight but it got a good but reluctant boost from the military. The army had been segregated since the Civil War. President Roosevelt signed an executive order prohibiting discrimination based on race or national origin in federal agencies but African American troops still remained in separate units. In 1948 President Truman issued an order which required equal treatment for all African Americans in the military. Many commanding officers ignored the order at first. It took well over a year to be fully implemented but by 1950, it was in effect. By 1953, the success of fully integrated fighting units of Marines in the Korean War with lack of visible racial tension between the soldiers finally convinced the Pentagon that a fully integrated military not only would work but was desirable.

The rest of society wasn't so smooth. By 1895, it was clear that Reconstruction had failed. A group of African American and Euro-American leaders in the South agreed to the Atlanta Compromise. African Americans led by Booker T. Washington of The Tuskegee Institute agreed that Blacks would not press their demands in return for consideration for education, jobs, and fair treatment under the law. This was "Separate But Equal" that became the foundation of segregation in the South for the next 60 years. It soon became clear that facilities would be separate but not equal. This is the way it was till the Supreme Court by a unanimous decision in 1954, struck down "Separate but Equal" in schools as unconstitutional. This was the modern civil rights movement which began with African Americans questioning the wisdom of the Atlanta Compromise. Under the leadership of W. E. B DuBois, the National Association of Colored People was created in 1909. It's mission "to ensure the political, educational, social, and economic equality of rights of all persons and to eliminate race-based discrimination".

The anti-Negro Klu Klux Klan had disbanded after the end of reconstruction but was revived in 1915 and had grown to considerable influence in the 1920's. The revived Klansmen were strict religious fundamentalists, anti-Roman Catholic, anti-Jewish and fanatic White Supremacists. They were probably responsible for many of the lynchings of the 1920's to the 1950's.

In 1955, Rosa Parks refused to give up her seat on a Montgomery, Alabama bus. Thus began the Montgomery bus boycott which lasted over a year and successfully challenged the old Jim Crow laws. In 1960, four African American college students sat at a Woolworth lunch counter in North Carolina and ordered coffee. They were ignored till closing. They came back two days later and thus began sit-ins that challenged segregation throughout the South. There was hostility. There was violence but Dr. Martin Luther King called for non-violence in the spirit of Mahatma Gandhi. Stokely Carmichael called for Black Power. These were turbulent times. There was great effort put into getting Black people registered to vote. In 1963, the Civil Rights March on Washington brought 250,000 people to the Lincoln Memorial to end segregation, end job discrimination and insure voting rights. Racial segregation which allowed job discrimination was the law in most Southern States and the norm in many areas of the North and West. The boycotts, sit-ins and freedom rides on interstate busses were effective and attracted violent resistance. The televised attacks by police dogs and firehoses on peaceful demonstrations in Birmingham Alabama and the murder of three civil rights workers (2 White, 1 Black) who were working to register voters in Mississippi, turned public opinion against those who resisted civil rights. In June, 1963 President Kennedy had announced in a televised address to the American People that he was sending a comprehensive Civil Rights Bill to Congress. After President Kennedy's tragic death, President Johnson promised to see the Bill through congress. After much resistance, the Civil Rights Bill of 1964 was signed into law on July 2, 1964.

The prosperity of the 40's and 50's brought better jobs and wages for some African, Asian, and Hispanic families while Native families were often left trapped on the reservations.

Many still remained stuck in neighborhoods with rundown housing, poor schools, drugs, alcoholism, and street gangs. There was often violence and abuse. This was an explosive situation. A pattern was emerging of run down inner cities surrounded by Euro-American suburbs. A new form of separate but not equal. Serious riots in Watts (LA 1965,) Detroit (1965,) and following the shooting death of Rev. Martin Luther King (1968) brought home the violent racial tension in the American people. President Lyndon Johnson had created a commission to investigate the causes of the urban riots and to make recommendations for the future. Under the direction of Governor Otto Kerner of Illinois, the report sited lack of economic opportunity, failed social services especially the police, and institutionalized, systemic racism as the cause of the violence and riots.

How do we change history? If we let it run its course, we will repeat the same cycles of compassion and violence. The tragic story will continue.

First…we must own history. It is who we are. We can't deny it. European people have created both a great civilization and committed great sins against humanity. African Americans, Native Americans, and Asian Americans have survived and triumphed against overwhelming odds. Something of which we can all be proud. Euro-Americans must own the great accomplishments of Western Civilization but stop thinking it as a norm for all of humanity. It is just one part of the great human story.

Euro-Americans should stop equating civilization with the color of skin. (Often sub-conscious, Euro-Centrism is thinking White, Western Civilization is the crown of human history.) We must realize that we are all part of the great story of emerging humanity and that we must change how we think if that story is to make it to the next level. There is only one human race. The DNA that makes us human is 99% the same the world over: the same heart, the same brain, the same lungs, the same skeleton, the same blood, the same emotions, the same gift for language and spirituality, the same ability to love and fear. We can love someone very different from us and have very human babies. The diversity is enormous but only on the surface. Skin color, hair texture, facial features, stature are minor variations of our Great Race. The closest species to us are chimpanzees whose DNA is 96% the same as ours. The last human species other than us, the Neanderthals, died out 27,000 years ago. There is only one human race on earth. But the variations are enormous. We can see that just by looking around. The chromosomes of breeding produce people of differing gifts, gender, color, abilities, and personalities. The accident of birth, history, environment, and culture can be both a plus and a minus. We all have to deal with that. Being human isn't easy. It's a challenge.

Second. We should stop thinking of race as skin color and start thinking of race as geography. We are African, European, Native, and Asian with many combinations of all the above. Each with our own story. When a White cop shoots a Black teenager in the back for shoplifting a box of cigars, it's not just racist but the subconscious sin of Euro-Centrism which is stuck to the bones of any one born White in America. That's why anyone born in America is a bit of racist to one degree or another. Euro-Americans must realize that and deal with it. The Euro Cop, whether he is aware of it or not, is acting from a subconscious script of defending society from someone who is seen as inferior. White bad guys are roughed up and arrested. Black bad guys are shot. This is the message of "Black Lives Matter." This is not easy. Think about it. White mass murders are cornered by the cops and arrested to stand trial. African American petty criminals are often shot dead. This is Euro-Centrism at its worse. It's the same script that justified slavery to many Southerners, that massacred Native and Asian peoples, and justified the lynchings, and creates an awkward, pervasive racial tension in our modern world. We can move beyond this.

All lives are precious—

To ease the pain,
We must not see people as color
But see people in their "story."
It's all our story.

We are all part of the Great Story—
In both its shame and the glory.

Amen and Blessed be—

THANKS FOR READING

I hope it was worth your while. This is a short history. There is so much more. I had to leave so much out. I invite you to continue the journey of learning about our **_Great Story_** and your part in it. There is so much out there in libraries, on-line, and even on You Tube and in stories told around the dinner table. Beware of ideas that are slanted or would turn one group against another. Those ideas will eventually doom themselves. The journey is our destiny and we are all a part of it.

Curran Jeffery

A Short History of Race in the Americas

For Young Readers Of All Ages

The author gives permission to quote from this work whenever and wherever its use may serve to further understanding between the peoples of the Americas.

Copies may be ordered from Amazon.com.

I invite you to make copies available to your local libraries, schools, churches, synagogues, mosques and temples.

Blessings,

Curran

ISBN 9798666834664

Made in the USA
Columbia, SC
15 November 2020

24619855R00019